MW01537852

This Book Belongs To:

____

Notes

Notes

Notes

Notes

Notes

Notes

Notes

Notes

Notes

Notes

Notes

Notes

Notes

Made in the USA
Las Vegas, NV
28 August 2021

29145971R00066